Oth

An introduction to Fairy, Elf & Angel Seeds

By Paul McCarthy

To contact the Author

You can contact the author by email at guidedbythelight@hotmail.com

Website: https://otherkin-fairyseeds.com/

The previous Books "Ascension, Spiritual Growth & Ascended Master", "Star Seeds, ET's & Star Beings" and "Learn to Channel your Guides" are available to purchase through Amazon.

Contents

Introduction

THIS IS A BOOK about fairy seeds, elf seeds and angel seeds. These are human beings who also have existence as fairies, elves and angels. The information is given to help them in understanding and embracing this beautiful reality. These fascinating people share the same qualities as these "mythical beings" from other realms. Often these qualities come with them to earth as it is a part of them and indeed forms the essence of what they are. I define these in detail so that the reader can recognise these traits and abilities. I do not write in general about fairies, elves and angels from other realms. There is a lot of good books about this already. My contribution is to explain what happens when they come to earth as human beings!

In the general chapters I simplify the descriptions by referring to the "seeds". These are the group that include fairy seeds, angel seeds and elf seeds. Of course, in the dedicated chapters I am talking just about the one being in question. Therefore in the angel seed chapter I am only talking about angel seeds and not fairy seed or elf seeds. Also I mainly write about three main categories (fairies, elves and angels), but I am not inferring that other groups do not exit. I am sure that there are others it is just that I can only write about that which I know and I mainly encounter these three groups. I have met a single dwarf seed and I instinctively feel that dragon seeds exist. I also sense that there are subgroups for each group but for the purposes of this book, I want to gently introduce this beautiful subject without turning it into a science.

1

Otherkin, Fairy Seeds, Elf Seeds and Angel Seeds

W E HAVE THE most amazing fairy tales describing fairies, elves, mermaids and other "mythical beings." Hans Christian Andersen and the Grimm brothers wrote about these beings long ago and yet these books are still as popular today as they have always been. Their stories captured the sense of magic and the mystery surrounding these beings which children and some adults can easily relate to. It is widely assumed that these stories are imaginary and yet as we will see later, there was the acknowledgement of these beings as being real in past writings and this subject has even shaped language itself.

Today the subject of fairies and elves are more popular than ever. There is currently a growth in fairy events where people dress up and celebrate all things fairy like. There are festivals, parties and magazines now dedicated to this subject. This activity transcends mere enjoyment of a fantasy. The love and fascination that these people have for such things point to a deeper acknowledgment of the reality of these beings and the desire to somehow reconnect to them.

Otherkin are a subculture who socially and spiritually identify as not entirely human. Some otherkin claim that their identity is genetic, while others believe their identity derives from reincarnation and soul ancestry. This group have only been active since 1991 and have websites and online groups dedicated to this subject.

I know that fairies, elves and angels are real as I sense their presence, energies and thoughts. I am a channel and a psychic and I am extremely sensitive to nonphysical realities. For me these other realities are just as real as the physical reality I see with my eyes. When I interact with them it is fascinating, revealing and spiritual in nature. As a new age channel and teacher I study all kinds of subjects like healing, crystals and spiritual growth and this has led to an exploration of the fairies, elves, angels, mermaids and unicorns etc. Like you I wanted to know all about them. What are they really like? Where are they? How do we humans find them and connect to them? What do they do? How can they help us? In my explorations and communications with them I answered these questions and learnt how to recognise the distinctive energies of the different groups of beings. With this new skill I then noticed something unexpected. These same energies were present in some of my clients that I was channeling for and teaching in my workshops! Some individual humans were carrying fairy energy or elf energy. The only way this is possible is if these people have existence in these other realms as well as being a human being on earth. I am used to this concept as this is the reality of star seeds who are humans who also have existence elsewhere in the universe as star beings and carry the star energies. This is why I call them fairy seeds or elf seed etc. They are in a sense "seeding" their gifts and qualities here on earth from these other realms. Not only that, I noticed that these individuals also exhibited the same qualities and gifts that I notice in the original beings. So, a fairy seed (a human who is also a fairy in the fairy realms) carries the energies of fairies and exhibits the qualities and gifts of fairies. I have written about the different qualities in the following chapters. Generally I find people only exist to one of these categories if at all. These qualities and gifts represent the core of these people. It is the essence of who they are and as they grow and shed the illusions of the human ego this is what is left. At a deep level these qualities motivate us to live in certain ways and to help others around us using the gifts we bring with us from these other realms. For anyone who is trying to discover the truth of their reality then this subject is very important. Those who are greatly attracted to fairies or angels are often tuning into this reality and are probably fairy seeds or angel seeds themselves. I have written this book to bring insight and direction to those who share this reality.

Otherkin refers to those who socially and spiritually identify as not entirely human. Some otherkin believe they have previous or parallel lives in other dimensions as one of the mystical beings and that they have reincarnated on earth as a human being. Others believe themselves as "trans species."

There is some similarity between those who identify as Otherkin and those who I call the seeds. They both basically acknowledge these other realms as being real and that they personally are linked to them. However I do not resonate with nor encourage others to get involved with physical transformations in order to make themselves physically look like dragons, fairies or whatever. There is some of this taking place in the otherkin community and it is not my way. My observation of true seeds is that they usually feel very different from other people and they spend a lot of time trying to find ways to fit in within a society. Their task is to blend these realties with their human reality in ways that make it work best for them and not to indulge in exaggerating the differences between them and others by radically altering the way they look to advertise these differences. My work is to teach others about these spiritual and energetic realities and not to encourage people to have plastic surgery.

What is the difference between a star seed and one of the seeds? They refer to different locations or realms where we also have existence. I find that the people I work with are often both star seeds and one of the seeds as well. I recommend that people explore both subjects. The fairy, angel and elf realms represent the true home of the seeds and that which they will ultimately return to. The star seed aspect represents lives lived in the stars on physical planets and light ships (but sometimes also in etheric realms). Their influence is reflected in how we operate when in a physical body (etheric Body), our practical gifts and the specific missions. For example a fairy seed with a Sirian star seed connection might also be an angel seed who seeks to liberate human from suffering (angelic) but uses the training methods of Sirius (healing and teaching) to achieve this.

I find that the different beings tend to favour destinations in the stars that resonate with their groups. For example I find elf and fairy seeds usually always have a connection to the Orion stars and particularly with Alnilam, Bellatrix and Alnitak. The angel seeds pop up in connection with Sirius and the mermaid seeds with Saiph in Orion.

2

Meeting Rhianna

I WAS WALKING DOWN the street thinking about connecting to the elves. In that instant my body felt as if I had turned into a very tall being. I struggled to walk normally as my body felt as if it belonged to someone else and I was looking down a long way to the pavement and my feet. I sensed this growing energy inside of me and knew that it was an elf that I had summoned through my thoughts. It was surprising to me even as an experienced channel as it was the first time that I had experienced this physical reaction to the encounter. In truth it was more like a paranormal event.

"My name is Rhianna and I am the Queen of the Elves" declared this being whose energy I was now merged with. I had not heard of an elf queen called Rhianna, only Rhianna the pop star. I was not seeing her but I could sense her presence as though she was inside of me. When I channel other types of beings, I sense them as being outside of me and so this was a first. Just like a queen she was calm, serene and majestic.

To start with she was quiet and only responded to my questions giving clear and direct answers. She explained much and confirmed my thoughts that I must be an elf seed myself. This was the first of many communication sessions. I love the way that she gets to the heart of a subject with such wisdom and with no hint of an ego only the sincere desire to help me.

I researched the name Rhianna and discovered it mean "queen" and so it made sense to me. I have since learnt that she is not THE QUEEN of the Elves. It is a human way of looking at things to expect one being to be in charge of all of the others. The reference to Queen here is more of a ceremonial title that describes her work in reaching out beyond the Elf Realms to help beings elsewhere such as on Earth. As such there are other "queens."

I now channel her for my clients in their readings and within my programmes. * I also ask her to give me information about the other types of beings such as fairies and angels etc. I know that there are connections between elves, fairies and unicorns but nevertheless she is as knowledgeable about the other non-elf species as her own. In a series of workshops on elves and fairies she helped me to teach people about the deeper realties of these beings and I have never seen as much excitement in any of my other workshops. There is such an amazing and longstanding connection between elves and humanity.

* Please see the chapter "What Next?"

Fairy Seeds

LIKE FAIRIES, fairy seeds are here to help others fulfil their potential and their Purpose. This is the most important statement in this chapter to explain the deeper nature of fairy seeds. Think of the deva that surrounds the flower and tends carefully to its energy needs at the etheric level. There is nothing more satisfying to a fairy seed than to help a friend, family member or client to embrace their potential and align to that they are really here to do. In doing this they use their ability to see through people's illusions and help others to connect to their true essence and at a deeper level to align to them to their universal purpose and the flow of energies that connect us to this. As such they can make great counsellors, mentors, life coaches or even psychics. Their amazing creative abilities can be used to put these efforts into the world in expanded ways through art, writing or through the media such as with films.

Fairy seeds can make good teachers as long as what they are teaching resonates with them. There are many different types of teachers. Some work with pure information and knowledge. This is not enough for fairy seeds who need to see their efforts work to enhance peoples lives and align them to their own truth and purpose. As such they need to carefully choose their teaching training and eventual work very carefully.

Fairy seeds can be healers. Their greatest gift is to re-align people to their true energies and purpose. This is a spiritual experience and so any kind of healing that is less technical and more spiritually aligned will suit them best. However fairy seeds need to be careful with all these potential jobs as if any situation prevents them from being themselves and instead calls them to experience too much negativity then they will struggle and possibly become depressed.

Fairy Seeds as a friend or family member

At their best fairy seeds can be spontaneous, funny, naughty and joyful. They have an enigmatic quality about them. Some even look fairy like and have an otherworldly aura about them. At their worst they can be angry, wild, stubborn and depressed. They are sensitive and need help in avoiding situations and people that are too harsh and that brings them down. They do have an ability to bounce back from such experiences but if there are too many of these it can lead to depression. Having a relationship with a fairy seed can be fun but you have to be prepared to give them a lot of room to be independent.

Unique Problems

Fairy Seeds have a difficulty with authority and institutions that impose structure on their lives and thoughts. They instinctively have an inner radar that guides them as to the true intentions and legitimacy of those they encounter. This can lead them to being wary of anyone trying to control them. They do however enjoy structures that genuinely support them. In general though structure and reality can crush them. They are after all sensitive and very creative and creative people need freedom not restrictions or to be dominated by the harsh realities of life.

Energy Needs

In terms of energy work, fairy seeds need to be really energised. They naturally need high levels of chi, prana & ka. They may benefit from an etheric infusion for this. They naturally benefit from environments where they connect to pure energies of nature such as forests and the seaside.

Fairy seeds thrive on creative energies. They enjoy people, places and situations where they can genuinely be creative and spontaneous.

The Dark side of Fairy Seeds

All of the seeds can be tested and challenged by life on earth. Despite coming to earth in order to help humanity, they can be led astray and fall into the same traps as everyone else. Indeed each category has its own vulnerabilities and "Achilles heel."

For fairy seeds the main spiritual test comes in the form of fitting into society at a human level. Out of all of the seeds they have the most defined ego and strongest sense of how things "should be" which comes from their instinctive sense of the fairy realms. They really only want to be themselves and do not want to change or compromise. Think of the Peter Pan character and it is similar to many fairy seeds. This is understandable but it does put them on a collision course with the world around them that tries to shape and mould them into different types of people. It can lead to rebellious and awkward behaviour as well as fairy seeds isolating themselves. This dynamic is even present with other spiritually orientated people such as older souls. Fairy seeds have often had less lives on earth as a human compared to the typical older soul type. As such they do not have the same type of dense energy fields. Indeed their energies are often clear and bright. They may not resonate with the older soul types whose experiences and energy fields are very different from their own.

The task for fairy seeds is to learn how to compromise with the world of humans enough to get on and have an ordinary life whilst still honouring their own needs and missions enough to feel alive and not crushed by their experiences.

Fairy Magic

Much is written about the ability of fairies to enact magic. There are many stories of fairies using enchantments, charms and spells to influence the lives of humans. The real magic of fairies is to connect humans to the natural flows of spiritual energies that exist and that shape our experiences of the physical world. These energies pull us into alignment with our inner truth, true purpose and natural abilities. You would think that people would automatically be like this? However we live in a world of free will and most human beings deny such realities and live a false existence devoid of spirituality and truth. As such we mostly exist outside of the natural flow of energies that seek to aid us. If called upon, fairies can help us to awaken us to such things and "plug us back." From our point of view when we are really connected in this way life flows in natural ways and we experience synchronicity, luck and we manifest in easier ways. We are "charmed" in a sense. Fairies love to help us in these ways. I have separate fairies working with me on different projects that I want help with to manifest.

Fairy seeds on earth also have this ability to help people in similar ways. It is not magic as such but the natural energies that radiate from fairy seeds. If this is combined with practical help it can be of great use to people. The power of this help cannot be underestimated. It can change lives and I dare say that some of the recipients of such transformations would claim it to be magical.

Where Fairy Seeds can best meet Fairies

So if you are a fairy seed then you will be missing the fairy realms and the fairies themselves. It is natural to be curious about them, seek them out, and to want to have some type of tangible connection with them. It is possible to set up a new age style meditation and to invoke their presence. This is what I do as a channel. I can provide you with attuned crystals that make this much easier if you do not have the skills, experience or confidence to do this for yourself.

If you want a more physical experience of this encounter then you go to those places where it is easier to sense the presence of fairies and the fairy realms. Fairies are of course not physical and this is why we do not usually see them with our physical eyes. I appreciate there are some unusual cases where some people claim to have seen them and photographed them. However these cases do not mirror most people's experiences which are more spiritual and more paranormal in quality. You know this to be true when you summon fairies and you can sense them but cannot actually see them with the physical eyes. They exist in the fairy realms which are more etheric in nature. So the real question is where can you more easily connect to the fairy realms? Many people enjoy being in the woods and forests where the presence of fairies is more obvious than in other places. But there are better places than this. Fairies can best be found in in-between places and at in-between times. I love this way of looking at this means the fairy kingdoms are not outside our reality but in-between or interpenetrating our reality. The elements of water, earth and air are important with this. With the elements, "in-between" is where land meets water and air such as at a waterfall or at the beach. And the best time is when daytime meets night time such as at dusk. Here dusk is in-between day and night. There is a powerful portal that opens at dusk where the fairy realms become much more obvious. You can even feel the energies building up to a climax. It is very exciting and it is my favourite time of day. I once invited the participants of my workshop to come out to a park to fully experience this. It was amazing and everyone could sense the different phases of this amazing portal opening.

Our Personal Fairy

All humans have a personal fairy whose role is to help us to fulfil our potential as humans but also as spiritual beings. It is important to acknowledge that to fairies everything is spiritual and the physical earth is just one part of this vast spiritual creation. Their aim therefore for us is to reach our spiritual potential and destiny. Where a person is not engaging with spirituality their personal fairy remains dormant and their own personal growth stagnates. Where someone is actively progressing with their spiritual growth their personal fairy also grows into an amazing fairy being. Their growth and experiences are directly related to ours. When I channel for spiritual people, their personal fairy often is full of love and gratitude to their human ward. By growing ourselves we give the fairies the opportunity to grow as well. Fairy seeds also have personal fairies as they are currently human too.

4

Elf Seeds

L IKE ELVES, elf seeds are here to help others by guiding them to the light. Light is the interactive intelligence and creative force of the divine. Elves in the elf realms are magnificent beings of light. Although modern fairy tales portray elves are being small and mischievous beings this is not a reality and they are actually the opposite. They possess noble, powerful and majestic characters. At their core the elf seeds too possess these qualities although they may be tested here in earth to stay true to these. An example of this was King Alfred the Great who as an elf seed possessed these qualities and hence is the only King of England to be called "great."

I have heard my guides describe elf seeds as incorruptible reflecting the deep respect all beings have for them. I myself have met some elves in my dream state and on one occasion I remember just crying in my sleep in their presence as their immense beauty was overwhelming. I think the portrayal of elves in the Lord of the Rings movies reflect these realities well. This combination of beauty and power is most interesting as here on earth we polarise everything so that we place power and beauty at opposite ends of the spectrum. However in the elf realms this duality does not really exist as we know it on earth. It is a heaven in many ways. Artists are often the closest in accurately portraying spiritual dimensions and so if you google "elf realms", in the images section you will see many magical and beautiful landscapes.

The true nature of elves was known to those in northern Europe over time. The European word "Alb" is connected by the idea of whiteness. The Germanic word presumably originally meant "white person", perhaps as a euphemism. Jakob Grimm thought that whiteness implied positive moral connotations, and noting Snorri Sturluson's ljósálfar, suggested that elves were divinities of light. Alaric Hall has suggested that elves may have been called "the white people" because they were regarded as beautiful. There is no racial element to this, only a crude effort to describe the beauty of these spiritual beings in older languages.

Indeed the reality of elves is shown in early European languages and stories. Old English names in elf-include the cognate of Alboin Ælfwine (elf-friend), Ælfric (elf-powerful), Ælfweard (elf-guardian) and Ælfwaru (elf-care). A widespread survivor of these in modern English is Alfred (Old English Ælfrēd, "elf-advice). Also surviving are the english surname Elgar (Ælfgar, elf-spear) and the name of St Alphege (Ælfhēah, elf-high). German examples are Alberich, Alphart and Alphere and Icelandic examples include Álfhildur. These names suggest that elves were positively regarded in early Germanic culture. Of the many words for supernatural beings in Germanic languages, the only ones used in personal names are elf and words denoting pagan gods, suggesting that elves were considered similar to gods.

In Skandiavia the mythical Norse gods refer to a realm called Alfheim and Enland (Britain) has been called Alboin. The connection between elves and England is probably the strongest one throughout history as illustrated by the existence of elf portals as described below.

Like elves in the elf realms, elf seeds on earth possess great abilities to work with spiritual energies. They are able to work with portals, attune energies, connect to and channel energies at will. They are also naturally sensitive, psychic and can channel well. Clearly this leads elf seeds to work in the new age movement as teachers, channels and energy workers. In other types of work, they are attracted to positions of leadership as they are known for being trustworthy and independently minded. They do have a creative side which they like to explore. Although not as natural and spontaneous as fairy seeds, it seeks to connect them closer to that which they intuitively seek for and yearn for which is the light and beauty of the elf realms.

Energetic Needs of Elf Seeds

Elf seeds need to be surrounded by highly spiritual energies and need the freedom to explore and enjoy the universe around them. Anything that prevents them from doing this will greatly frustrate them and lead them to despair. There is a distant memory in the hearts of elf seeds of an existence where there is unlimited freedom to do what you want and be who you want. The restrictions placed on physical humans greatly puzzle them and annoy them. Elf seeds inevitably become attracted to the new age movement as it promises them liberation from the ignorance and constraints of the human condition. They instinctively know there is much more to reality than they are being shown as a human being. They are after all mighty light beings in the elf realms. Ultimately elf seeds possible have the greatest potential to embrace the unseen spiritual and energetic realities as it is their existence back home in the elf realms. As such they need to embrace and use the best that the new age movement has to offer in order to awaken this part of them and allow them to thrive as human elf seeds. Indeed they have the potential to go well beyond what human teachers can teach them if they develop and test themselves.

The Dark side of Elf Seeds

All of the seeds can be tested and challenged by life on earth. Despite coming to earth in order to help humanity, they can be led astray and fall into the same traps as everyone else. Indeed each category has its own vulnerabilities and "Achilles heel." For elf seeds the main spiritual test comes in the form of their relationship to power.

In the elf realms, elves are highly evolved spiritual beings and possess a lot of power. Power normally sits well with them as they are generally immensely trustworthy and dedicated to the light. In the elf realms this is not tested. Coming to earth as human beings they are stripped of all power and tested in all ways. Invariably they do well as their instinct to be virtuous guides them well. However, they are tested in the following ways:

They are attracted to power as it feels right to them. Usually this attraction is to the benefits power brings and allows them use for others. However, where a lifetime of subconsciously searching for anything that feels like home, leads an elf seed towards a negative form of power that appears to offer resolution, an elf seed can allow themselves to be seduced by it. Here they can allow themselves to be confused by the illusions of power in order to gratify the feelings of gaining the freedom they have been searching for. They can be tested by the dark side of power which is the selfish use of power that can take away the free will of others. Often this is a test they pass as in the hearts of elf seeds they want to empower and serve others and this drive is hard to derail.

The second test comes in the form of friction in relationships. Some people subconsciously sense the nobility and power of elf seeds. For those who are uneasy about their own relationship to personal power, the presence of an elf seed can trigger this unresolved part of self. These individuals project this issue into the relationship by creating dramas centred around power. They might unfairly challenge their authority or try to undermine them. Here an elf seed might find themselves in the middle of a conflict that they did not start or even want. Dealing with jealous and irrational people will be normal for elf seeds.

Where Elf Seeds can best meet Elves

So if you are an elf seed then you will be missing the elf realms and the elves themselves. It is natural to be curious about them, seek them out, and to want to have some type of tangible connection with them. It is possible to set up a new age style meditation and to invoke their presence. This is what I do as a channel. I can provide you with attuned crystals that make this much easier if you do not have the skills, experience or confidence to do this for yourself.

If you want a more physical experience of this encounter then you go to those places where it is easier to sense the presence of elves and the elf realms. Elves are of course not physical and this is why we do not usually see them with our physical eyes. Elves have created portals on earth that connect earth to the elf realms for the purpose of brining the light from that place here. Elves are totally focused on light and so this activity defines them well. If you are an elf seed and you stand close to one of these portals you will feel the power, grace and beauty of the energies emerging from the portal. It will feel like home and you will not want to leave. For elves and elf seeds the relationship to this energy is everything and relationships with other elves are less important. Hence you will not necessarily find elves coming through to you there unless of course you deliberately invoke them. There is one such portal in Brighton (southern England) on the beach in a specific location. Brighton is a very special place and although it is popular with tourists many do not understand its deeper attraction. The area of Brighton was once a part of Atlantis and carries a great spiritual and healing energy. It was the northern tip of a large area we call Atlantis which stretches down to the Azores in the Atlantic Ocean and includes parts of the coast of France and Spain. A great flood submerged much of Atlantis underwater, but the energies of Atlantis still exist today and you can feel them in Brighton. Is it any wonder why the Prince Regent built the Pavilion in Brighton and encouraged healing. Since then Brighton has attracted many who seek healing and today Brighton attracts many new age spiritual people and legions of therapists and healers just as it did in the times of Atlantis. I know that other portals exist in the large area we call Atlantis and there are possibilities in the Isle of White off of southern england. I have not travelled to these other parts of Atlantis and so cannot confirm exact locations at this moment. There are probably more elf portals in the world and so if you are an elf seed you will probably find them! The trick is to go to those places where you feel incredibly alive and love the atmosphere. Perhaps you will be tuning into a local elf portal.

5

Angel Seeds

LIKE ANGELS, angel seeds are here to save others and to be the embodiment of divine love and compassion._They are often caring, loving and selfless. Their capacity to open their hearts to others with compassion is truly divine in nature. They carry the saviour energies which motivates them to want to save other in great need. This is why many of them gravitate to nursing, social work and therapeutic activities. Their courage and ability to be selfless means that they often go into the darkest places to find and save others. They are attracted to working in the fields of drug abuse, alcoholism, mental health and hospice work. In the new age movement, they can be found working as healers and therapists (especially the talking therapies). Their ability to heal wounded hearts and reconnect people spirituality are their greatest gifts.

Angel seeds are often the embodiment of divine love. This means not only are they profoundly loving but they demonstrate this love through their actions. They truly walk their talk. They are often doing the work of angels as angel seeds in real life with their choice of work and in relationships.

Unique problems

Angel seeds express the saviour energies in a strong way. It is in their DNA to want to save those who are lost, in pain and those in their darkest hour. What else would you expect an angel to want to do? These are very special qualities and for this reason angel seeds really stand out. However where the impulse to do this is out of control then it can lead to difficulties for angel seeds. If an angel seed cannot discern when enough is enough or value their own needs as much as the needs of others then life for them can be chaotic and problematic. Are they entering into romantic relationships because it is the right relationship for them or because they sense the other person needs saving? Are they constantly trying to "fix" family, friends and dates? Whilst it is a tremendous to reach out and help people that approach leads angel seeds to miss out on having good relationships as those they spend time with can be more like therapy clients than genuine friends or romantic mates. A balance and a system are needed to protect their own energies and requirements. Perhaps they can do this work in a professional capacity but outside of this they can focus also on their needs.

Some angel seeds suffer extreme sensitivity. This means that most other people's energies feel too harsh to them and they upset their own sense of wellbeing. It can include a sensitivity to the energies and atmosphere of places. Symptoms of this hypersensitivity include feeling drained and exhausted, confused and lost as well as anxiety and fear. Such angel seeds must realise that they have to manage their sensitivity and avoid people, places and situations that cause them problems. They also need to appreciate their sensitivity and use it in positive ways. For example a sensitive nature works well for artists, musicians, writers and channels / psychics. Choices exist that support these sensitive angel seeds. If being physically present with people is hard, then they can work in a remote fashion instead which protects their energies more.

Energy Needs

Out of all of the seeds it is the angel seeds that feel most out of place on earth. The difference between the angelic realms and earth is greater than with elf and fairy seeds and their respective realms. There is a longing to return home within angel seeds that is profound and yet many are unaware as to what this really represents. Angel seeds need to be connected to angelic energies and ultimately to god or source (whatever you want to call this.) They really need to sense this aspect of home and to be nurtured by it. Angel seeds must use new age meditations to connect to angelic energies.

Where Angel Seeds can best meet Angels

Angels are less tied to the earth plane than elves and fairies. They are more universal by nature that the other types of beings. As such there are not the same "hot spots" on earth where you can go to connect to them as I have described for the other beings. It is true that that it is easier to sense angels in the northern hemisphere and especially in the northern countries of Scandinavia. This is why more of the folklore about angels, as we define them in the west, comes from the northern hemisphere. This enhanced receptivity however is general in nature. As such the "meeting place" for angels is to invoke them. Angels can connect to us wherever we are on earth. I find angels close to angel seeds as their purity attracts them and they often work through them even when angel seeds are unaware of this. The frequency of angels is so high that they usually can only work through those who are purer and carry a high vibration as a human. Also where there is service work (helping people) there is often angels present and especially is the activity connects to the spiritual realms such as with healing or at a hospice.

The Dark side of Angel Seeds

As mention above the great longing for home inside of angel seeds needs to be satisfied. If an angel seed cannot do this through helping people and by connecting to the angel realms then they will often go on a quest to find something to "plug the hole" inside of them. They see humans do this by abusing alcohol, drugs and sex and so may get pulled into a cycle of negativity in an attempt to dull the pain and in search of the highs that these things promise by ultimately do not deliver.

There is also a deep desire inside angel seeds to be as human as everyone else. They sense that they are not the same as others and desperately want to experience the same things that other people do. Their love of humanity is so great that they want to be human too, warts and all. Some angel seeds may feel that one way of doing this is to join in with all things in life including the negativity of people. This collusion with negativity manifests itself as the action of aligning with negative people and being a part of the drama that follows.

6

Others

Mermaid Seeds

I have only met one mermaid seed on earth and so I have not had enough opportunity to observe these beings as much as the ones in previous chapters. I think that their role was more relevant in the past than it is now. I know that the mermaids themselves are different from the stories we have on earth. For me these amazing beings are physical and their role is to create and open energy portals which they do by emitting a powerful vibration from an organ in their chest area. It is inaudible to human ears as it is so deep. They are sea creatures and they do in a sense "sing" and so I agree with these aspects of mythology. They come to young planets as mermaids in the earlier times in order to create portals. They originally come from a planet in the Saiph star system in the Orion constellation. The one mermaid seed that I met on earth was involved in creating mini portals using attuned vibrational essences. And so it seems that they were using their mermaid approaches one again in this world as a human mermaid seed.

Unicorn Seeds

As with mermaids, I have only met one unicorn seed on earth and so I have not had enough opportunity to observe these beings as much as the ones in previous chapters. For me unicorns are highly spiritual beings that are nonphysical and exist in etheric realms. They represent ceremonial guardians that come to us in those rare moments when we pass spiritual tests and initiations. They are the universal witnesses to our spiritual achievements. They work with elves and follow the light that comes from the elf realms to earth.

Unicorns have reputation for being elusive as their participation in human affairs is so unusual. The one unicorn that I did meet did indeed fulfil this mermaid role as a human mermaid seed by ushering in periods of transformation and initiations for others.

7

What next?

If you believe that you too are one of the seeds then maybe you want more help with this? Perhaps you identify strongly with one of the descriptions and you may want confirmation about this and to ask other questions?

Elf, Fairy, Angel Seed Personal Readings

In this reading Paul will channel his guide Rhianna Queen of the Elves for you. He will give information about any possible connection you have with the Fairies, Elves, Angels etc as well as giving personal guidance about how you can weave this reality into your life and deal with any problems this creates. This Fairy Reading and Angel Reading is about you.

All readings are sent to you as a digital file (either MP3 or .wma file) via email when the reading is completed. You can listen to this on a PC, Ipad or even a smart phone. This is a remote reading completed when Paul is receptive to channeling. There is no skype, no telephone call and no appointment necessary.

You are free to ask 2 additional questions of your choice. These may or may not be related to the content of the reading.

I also offer many themed readings which you can also book including, Star Seed, Ascension, Life Missions, Life Between Lives, Children's Reading, Aura Evaluation, Crossroads, Your Tribe & Last Life Reading.

You can contact me using the contact information below to arrange this.

Please note that my readings are popular and there is often a waiting list of about one to four weeks before a reading can be completed after payment. As such if you want a reading it is best that you book as soon as possible in order to receive it as soon as is possible.

Elf, Fairy, Angel Seed Programme

If it has already been confirmed that you are one of the seeds and if you want additional help in blending this reality with your human reality then you may wish to join the Elf, Fairy, Angel Seed Programme. This is a monthly programme where I channel and send you specific meditations, techniques and approaches that will help you to reconnect to these realities and make connections with beings from these other realms. I also channel personal guidance related to the programme for you. The programme is only available to elf, fairy or angel seeds.

Many Otherkins feel that there is not information or guidance available to them. If you research the internet you will find of lot of misleading and contradictory information about these subjects. As a result there are a lot of myths, incorrect and false information floating around the internet. As an elf seed myself and a channel I have managed to reconnect to the truths of these realities and I share these in my workshops and readings. However I recognise that Otherkins want precise, specific guidance and help. They want to reconnect to the training they have received in other lives and in other realms. They are ambitions and feel they instinctively know there is more to reality and their abilities than they remember or which is being taught to them by many teachers now on earth. After many requests I am now offering bespoke and focused help to Otherkins.

The programme provides meditations and techniques that work with your energies and consciousness. It requires you to repeatedly practice these, have some awareness of the realities involved, be open to change aspects of yourself and to be determined and patient. You need to follow the programme every month and so you need some time to invest in yourself. This typically might be 4 or more hours a month.

I will channel precise information for you about your development and what guidance Rhiannna has specifically for you. On alternative months, I can channel feedback after you have had time to practice the techniques. Also I can answer questions as Paul as I have a lot of experience of working with the same material and also as a teacher and writer. I can offer Q&A sessions and channeling for you. The plan is for me to work once every month with you and I send you either one channeling, or one channeling feedback or one Q&A session.

You can contact me using the contact information below to arrange this.

Paul's Otherkin website - https://otherkin-fairyseeds.com/

Paul's email – guidedbythelight@hotmail.com

I hope to help you with a reading or the programme.

Paul McCarthy

Printed in Great Britain
by Amazon